AF430332

寒　山

入矢義高 注

編集・校閲

吉川幸次郎
小川環樹

中國詩人選集 5

寒山の新詩集

No Mountain:
Improvisations from Han-Shan's
New Home in Ueno Park
Tokyo

recorded by
Wayne Pounds
Amanuensis
begun Dec. 2019
finished Mar. 2020

Acknowledgment:

Cover photo and design by Shelley Pounds, age sixteen.

Books of Poetry by Wayne Pounds

Following the Serpent (1984)
*Proletarian Life: Twenty Poems of Love Hate and
        Politics in the Capital of Texas* (1987)
San Luis Obispo Afternoons and Other Disasters (1989)
The Greater Deep Fork Navigation Project (1998)
Oklahoma Elegies: Chronicles and Family History
        (2011)
*The Pond: Poems from Tokyo's Ueno Park and
        Shinobazu Pond* (2011)
Along the Kaw: Poems 1968-1978. Vol. I of *By the
        Rivers of Edo* (2018)
Crossing on the Hankyu Meatwheel: Poems 1978-1989.
        Vol. II of *Rivers of Edo* (2019)
Child Nine: Auguries and Ashes, 1990-2003. Vol. III of
        By the Rivers of Edo (2019)
Into Blue Mountains: Poems 2004-2018. Vol IV of *By
        the Rivers of Edo* (2019)

Table of Contents

He Spoke and I Wrote

Like most poetry lovers who are also readers of
English, I first came across the Tang Dynasty poet Cold
Mountain in the pages of Gary Snyder, but Snyder is a
strong poet, so once I had conceived my own project I
put him aside and have not looked at him since. I even
stopped using the name Cold Mountain and in my mind
he lived under his Chinese name, Hanshan. Because I
live in Japan, I also called him Kanzan. He is especially
loved by the Japanese, who know him under that name.
Both of these names are readings of the characters 寒山.

Instead of Snyder, I might have first picked up
Kerouac's *Dharma Bums*, published in 1958 but
probably written soon after 1955, the year the novel
recounts. It was also the year that Snyder began his
translation. The legendary Chinese poet was a
sympathetic figure for the Beat Generation. In the
introduction to his translation which appeared in
the Evergreen Review, Snyder wrote of Hanshan, "He
and his sidekick Shih-te (Jittoku in Japanese) became
great favorites with Zen painters of later days — the
scroll, the broom, the wild hair and laughter. They

13

became Immortals and you sometimes run into them today in the skidrows, orchards, hobo jungles, and logging camps of America." Kerouac's The Dharma Bums closes with a vision of Hanshan, and at Snyder's suggestion, Kerouac dedicated the book to the poet.

It is the image of Hanshan as a Beat poet that has primarily appealed to me. Without ever intending to be one, and certainly without joining any of the Beat organizations which nowadays flourish on line, I have been a Beat poet all my life, both beaten down and blessed, though never beatified.

For twenty years now I have lived a ten-minute walk from Shinobazu Pond in Tokyo's Ueno Park. This whole area was once the Kan'ei-ji 寛永寺 temple complex, and much of it still is, including the lotus pond with its magnificent plants flowering from the primal mud of existence and symbolizing Buddhist paradise. Perhaps six months ago I became intrigued with a tiny circular island on the north side of Benzaiten 弁財天, the central shrine. It is kept locked except on Snake Days, once every twelve days as figured by the old Chinese sexagenarian reckoning. Benzaiten is one of the Seven Gods of Good Fortune 七福神 in Japan, and her father was a white snake. Thus, the gate to this tiny island, called Shōtenjima / 聖天島, opens only on Snake Days.

Of the many stone memorials on the island, two especially captured me, a statue of En no Gyōja 役行者,

legendary founded of the Yamabushi 山伏, and the broken figure of a *Kōshin* 庚申, a name that defies translation, since his cult was banned in the Meiji Era and has died out, but a kind of god or guardian of crossroads and gates. Surprisingly it warrants an article in Wiki, where it is described as a "a folk faith in Japan with Taoist origins, influenced by Shinto, Buddhism and other local beliefs."

> A typical event related to the faith is called Kōshin-kō (庚申講), held on the Kōshin days that occur every 60 days in accordance with the Chinese sexagenary cycle. On this day some believers stay awake to prevent Sanshi (三尸), entities believed to live inside the body of believers, from leaving it during that night in order to report the good and specially the bad deeds of the believer to the god . . .

The point should be taken that this is a folk religion with no hierarchy or formal organization. The cult was banned but the stone images remain, and they exist across the whole of traditional Japan (i.e., excluding Okinawa and Hokkaido.) With the widening of roads during the Meiji Era, the images were moved to undisturbed areas, often to the grounds of a nearby shrine.

15

**Koshin, unbroken figure showing the amanojaku
and the three monkeys under his feet**

The island of Shotenjima

Walk through the *torii* 鳥居 seen above, and the Kōshin figure is on the far left, as is that of his companion En no Gyōja. A scholar of Japanese history and archaeology visited the island once, examined the statue, and told me that the stone was from the Jōmon Era. It has facial features now, and hands and feet, but originally it was a phallus, as everyone recognizes who sees it from behind. At some time the hands, feet, and face, were chiseled into the original phallus, probably by Meiji Era puritans who were embarrassed by vestiges of

17

what they considered "paganism." En faces outward, toward the water, as do almost all the stones on the island, reflecting the fact that it could only be approached by boat because no bridge had yet been built. This was the era when "tea houses" lined the banks of the pond on the Ueno Mountain side, such houses serving for assignations between prostitutes and their clients. These were customers who would likely have been much titillated by En's shape.

The shape of the Kōshin is also not without interest. He treads on a poor devil known as a *jaki* or Amanojaku 天邪鬼. Underneath this downtrodden figure are three monkeys--speaking-, seeing-, hearing-no-evil-- everywhere part of the Kōshin iconography. Part of the monkeys' popularity over the centuries is surely due to a delicious pun in Japanese. The word for monkey, *saru*, is also a negative verbal suffix, so that negated "see" (*miru*) becomes *mizaru*; negated "hear" (*kiku*) becomes *kikazaru*; and negated "speak" (*iu*) becomes *iwazaru*. The three *zaru (*monkeys) with their negative imperatives must have helped control vicious gossip, the bane of village life.

Into the island's rich historical broth, I decided to immerse Han Shan, that is insert him imaginatively by giving him a spiritual home there. He seemed happy enough with the idea and over the next two months gave me a total of fifty short verses, which you now hold in your hands. Whatever these verses are, they are not translations. I think of them rather as homages, instigations, and provocations inspired by my reading of Han Shan.

As I say, I have avoided Snyder, and that means I've not touched any of the thirty poems he translated, but Han Shan is credited with some three hundred poems, so I still had plenty left for my instigations. My sources have been primarily two, a standard Japanese translation of the poems (an image of the book provides the front flyleaf), and Red Pine's *The Collected Songs of Cold Mountain*. Both of these are cited in my "Sources" and both are academic translations, well done and excellent in their accuracy but not inspiringly poetic. I have profited most from Red Pine's notes, which are lengthy and detailed and often sparkle with glints of gold panned from his historical researches.

These poems came to me in such an abundance over a two-month period that I felt less like a poet and more like an amanuensis. Somehow Han Shan began to speak to me, and I wrote down what I heard. In my years by Ueno Park, I've come to call myself Ueno Wayne, both for the word play and for fine nuance that is felt when a poet calls himself by the name of the place that inspires him. I've had to give a new name to Han Shan's place of residence as well, and since what the Japanese are pleased to call Ueno Yama 上野山 is no mountain at all but rather a good sized hill, my Han Shan also uses the moniker No Mountain.

The pun for No Mountain is obviously Noh Mountain but I've avoided it and the reader too should rid his mind of it. If anything, we should think of Donovan. "First there is a mountain, then there is no mountain, then there is." Han Shan was not a zen monk. He was not any kind of Buddhist monk, for he liked to get drunk. He wasn't a man of Zen either, but from our perspective today he may seem like one. He offers no precepts (though he does like to moralize) but represents a practice, and that practice, we can say, was zen-like. Red Pine is clear on this matter: "Certainly his poems reflect an understanding of both [Buddhism and Taoism], and he has been claimed by both orders. But he poked fun at Buddhists as much as at Taoists and presented himself as a man free of spiritual conceit, whatever its name" (14-15). Little is known about his life except legends. As he remarks in one of my poems, "It is not even certain I ever lived but my poems do."

What follows are the poems spoken by No Mountain as recorded by his amanuensis Ueno Wayne. Usually No Mountain responds to the world of the pond, but sometimes he gets topical, talking about the Monju nuclear plant, Prime Minister Abe, the corona virus, and other corporate disasters like Tokyo's Drunk Poets. He can't help it. He reads newspapers and he listens to people talk. The final poem, "No Mountain Bids Farewell," was his last poem. After that he visited me no more.

Wayne would like to hear from any readers who would care to write him: poundsway@gmail.com.

Tokyo, 1 April 2020
the day before his 74th birthday
the year of the Corona Virus

Forty-Nine Poems
by
No Mountain

They called me Cold Mountain--Hanshan in Chinese
and with the same strokes (寒山) Kanzan in Japanese
That's what I used to say but now I've changed
My name is now No Mountain

When I heard that in the 50s Jack Kerouac
in *The Dharma Bums* had made me
the guardian angel of the San Francisco Renaissance
I laughed so hard I had a piss attack

Karma is a tree of which we know only inches
its catches have numberless roots and branches

People ask the way to No Mountain
They ask the way to No Pond
There is no mountain, no pond
The highrises surround the whole

Two ridges, Ueno and Hongo*, and between them a dip
the ocean here ten thousand years ago
Withdrawing left a tidal flat, a slough
the water now murky and without depth

And you, sir, you could wade across it
and not wet your crotch

*上野 / 本郷

Passing through 黄泉 Yellow Springs

Once I reached Cold Mountain I stayed
thirty years, a price on my head and a gimp
I hobbled on big wooden clogs unfit
for service to the army or the state

Later I passed through 黄泉/Yellow Springs
land of the dead named for the sulfuric rock
when the earth opens and the water boils out
centuries I loitered on Mount Taishan

now I've floated to Shinobazu Pond
known for its lotus flowers
that rise from the muddy bottom
images of Buddhist paradise

This isle's called Hermits' Rest but I'm not
Master Kung*, not the teacher but the taught

* Confucius

They named the nuclear plant もんじゅ / Monju
after Mañjuśrī the bodhisattva of wisdom
an easy name to recall for kids
who all know the sweet-bean pastry *o-manju*

You all should make plans to visit sometime
The road won't get you into the plant
but you can see Japan the Beautiful hanging
on the the northern tip of the Tsuruga Peninsula

Two hours by bus from Kyoto or Osaka
and within spitting distance of Amanohashidate
one of the Japan's three great beauty spots
I'll tell you how to view Amanohashidate

You turn your back to it, then bend over
look at it upside down from between your legs
this makes you loopy so that the bridge appears
to be floating upwards, and it brings good luck

Now keep your head down and swivel 180 degrees.
Off toward the sea is the plant, floating to heaven
Just the sight's enough to start a fever in your bones

and turning again keeping your dipsy head down

there in the near distance shines beautiful Lake Biwa
drinking water for 8 million thirsty souls.

22 Dec. 二の巳 (*ni no mi*)[1]

Today my island's new gates were open
visitors clapped hands dropped coins in my offertory
a scholar of ancient things showed up
and was snapping photos of En no Gyoja 役行者
talking about sangaku bukkyo and shugendo[2]

En's the lucky one, his statue stone
from the Jomon Era, recut in Edo
or by the puritans of Meiji to make face and hands
originally he was a phallus, a hooded daikon

a male principle matched across the water
by the female spring that feeds the pond
Bentenzai's father was a white snake
Thus the island only opens on snake days

You need to be here for the summer solstice
it all lines up and the sun stands still

------

1. 二の巳 (ni no mi): the second snake day of the month
2. 山岳仏教 / 修験道

You can't see through the murk
Though the ducks love it, divers and dabblers
Its private parts are a muddy pudendum
sheathed with lotuses' great leaves

They cup the waterdrops that roll
when the wind raises their skirts
and the sunlight makes diamonds
No depth means no mystery but the muddy floor

No knowledge is gained here, no nothing
to know the mystery is to write on water
And what is water asked the poet
but the generated soul hereafter

Cosmeticians of Culture 

The culturata are giving my island a facelift
The jingle of go-en-dama will increase
do I need five-yen coins[3] rattling my offertory box
I don't know whether to be pissed or pleased

The facelift means first a new fence
fencing me in or fencing me out matters nay
The Tao that can be tao-ed is not the Tao
the way that can be weighed is not the way

Like the surgery they performed on my sidekick
En no Gyoja was a Jomon Era giant dick
then the Meiji puritans worked him over
giving him hands, a face, and feet

There never was a road to No Mountain
don't they know it's a place in the heart

---

3. Go en (五円) is a homophone with go-en (御縁), "en" meaning a
karmic tie or relationship, and "go" showing respect. Five-yen coins
are commonly given as donations at Shinto shrines with the
intention of establishing a good link with the deity of the shrine.

A Dream of the West

In my country the Central one you call China*
ancient graves were plowed into fields
I dreamed a Shangri-La land called America
where they didn't have the sense to burn bodies
they housed the dead above ground
covered them with bark to let their spirits rove
White rags on poles, the rooting hogs ate the corpses
These were a great people men with red skin

but pale skins had come and conquered them
and taught them the Great Spirit was a Jew
Even in China we'd heard of the great Hebrew
but that the Great Spirit belonged to one folk
was such a novelty I laughed when I awoke
Follow your ancestral gods
else flies will be your funeral guests
and your dead will be eaten by hogs

* In Japanese the word for China is written 中国, central
country.

The Year's First Mirror

Today was the first day of the year
the gates to our island standing open,
we two gods hovering for oblation
counting the goodies not the coins

Nagaoka Misue-dono may her name be blessed
left us a liter of sake in a New Year's box
we don't imbibe merely inhale the moving spirits
like the sweet smoke rising from incense

On our central shrine they left *kagami mochi*
two flat rice cakes with a mikan cap for color
and broken Road Guardian, missing two arms
still has four to receive a five-yen coin at his feet

初鏡　秘めごとのなく　拭き浄め[4]

the year's first mirror / nothing here hidden / all's wiped
clear

———————————

4. The haiku is from Jakucho / 寂聴 (Setouchi Harumi) in an NHK
haiku contest twenty years ago. My translation.

Buddha-izers, Confucians, and Tao-izers
they all thought they were hot spit
they only agreed upon their scorn
for the scrolls the others had writ

Came then in the long twilight of my day
a poet by the name of Ezra
who couldn't read Chinese but had a good ear
He translated Kung 君 into English

thinking to silence the harvest thieves*

They said of him, *non era confuciano ma confusionario*
they also called No Mountain a confusionist
but No Mountain says this
when they die they'll meet Old Yama
and he'll stick a hot broom handle up their butts

* "Stealers of harvests" was Pound's expression for bankers.

Here we languish, a pair of poor scholars
En no Gyoja 役行者 and I

His followers, yamabushi 山伏, bring him gifts

Golden Bat cigarettes and One-Cup sake
He's Mr. Austerity so he gives them to me
Who now share the same pond
once swam in different seas

No work now, but when did I ever work
I only throve in poetry and song
In my youth I was a scholar pinched by poverty
Now here I am again, living on five-yen coins
But the delights of the soul are free

Ueno Wayne claims that's his story too
now living on the nickels of retirement pay
Scribble, scribble, we wore out our brains
We could have written our poems on biscuits
The dumpster dogs wouldn't stoop to nibble

Golden Bat since 1906

En no Gyoja / 役の行者 / Isle of the Hermit's Haven (1)

Famous nowadays as the founder of the yamabushi
though such an anarchic bunch had no founder
it was just a prehistoric, mountain-and-bear worship
that may have started in western Wakayama

Today the yamabushi smoke those Golden Bat cigarettes,
super lethal at a twenty-five milligrams of tar each
What the hell, just another way
of practicing the austerities

Myself I take *kumazasa* 熊笹

the mountain bear bamboo-grass
powdered it restoreth my soul--that is, my liver--
and lets me continue the austerities of drink

精選濃縮　健康食品
ホシ　隈竹　エキス
くま　ざさ
国産クマ笹100％使用
星製薬株式会社

En no Gyoja 役行者 (2)

The rain beaten eyes see nothing,
the nothing that is and the nothing that is not
From behind, his silhouette is boldly phallic
attracting tipsy couples from the teashops
all during Edo 江戸 and Meiji 明治
Though they had to take a boat to get there
its shape was erect and erotic

He contemplates the stalking egret--
Oh, he has birds galore,
for the Ueno Zoo is there next door--
and the dawn moon sails white between the high rises
In late summer walking past this part of the pond
I hear the lonely boom of a bullfrog
seeking a mate, but the frogs have grown few
poisoned by mankind who cannot

stop ravaging and uprooting
until naught remains, not even frog spawn

En no Gyoja / 役の行者 / Hermit's Island (3)

Walking all the way from Wakayama
following Omine, the great ridge
to stand on a low island in Ueno Park
a grand enuff name--聖天島,

Holy Heaven Island you would think, but the 聖

is for *hijiri*, a yamabushi master.
En no Gyoja, En the hermit, En the way-walker.
Widely venerated, up until the end of Meiji.
He walks and walks
like the great egret stalks and stalks

Omine's forty-mile ridge of forest and streams
was En's original zendo. Thus no trick
to walk the many days from Zao Zao Gongen
Mountain King's home, to Ueno, no home,
but En didn't talk, he just walked
walking was the Way he taught
like Jesus and Socrates he wrote nothing down

En no Gyoja 役行者 / Shōtenjima 聖天島 / Holy
Hermit's Isle (4)

En no Gyoja's isle's the heart of Ueno Park
It's not in the guidebooks that tourists beguile
The stillest place, it's open only on snake days
to understand which will require you to study
a bit of the Chinese zodiac and Taoism.
goddamn your eyes, old Ezra liked to say

En's walking's ended now
His features eroding
He stares across the water
Ducks on the pond--
Life goes on

Chiisa no, heibon na shiawase de ii
A small, ordinary happiness suffices

En no Gyoja's Memorial Stone
役行者の石碑

Partial to penises and erotic display
the couples from the teahouses came to see it--
during Edo that was, before the bridges
you could only get here by boat

That's why every tribute stone
on the island faces the water
including En no Gyoja's
himself the founding phallus

I heard a scholar say his stone is Jōmon
that the face and hands were incised in Edo
this sounds to me like speaking of what is not
like counting the growth rings in a rock

En no Gyoja seen from the rear

Houses and Drones 

No Mountain's the secret name of this place
my home was here from the outset
long years before I ever heard the name
the place was already set in my heart

A pond-side house with no roof or walls
no place for a hazmat drone to land
carrying hot sand from Fukui's reactor
Save that for the Prime Ministerial mansion

I bow in respect to Yamamoto Yasuo
who flew one onto Czar Abe's roof
his residential workplace and office
where it rested two weeks without notice

In court he dressed like the homeless and me
gray sweatshirt and sweatpants, kulack not czar
They put him in the big house
the one with the door locks and window bars

In an April 2015 incident, a Phantom 2 drone carrying traces of radiation was found on the roof of the PM's office. It was controlled by Yamamoto Yasuo, an anti-nuclear protester from Fukui Prefecture. Yamamoto flew the drone containing cesium from Fukushima prefecture on April 9. He flew it out of a parking lot near the Prime Minister's Office in Chiyoda Ward and intentionally landed it on the roof of the building.

The drone was equipped with flares and a container filled with radioactive soil and affixed with a radiation sticker. It was discovered by officials nearly two weeks later on April 22. Yamamoto appeared at the court in a gray sweatshirt and sweatpants. He received a two-year suspended sentence

森羅万象 / *shinra bansho*: the whole of creation

I chose a hut between two ridges
surrounded by high-rise apartment houses
What remains is an island in a lotus pond
Ducks, both divers and dabblers, a lonely stone.

I have lived here unknown for ages
riding the carousel of the seasons
now Abe Shinzo rules *shinra bansho*
from his Prime Ministerial suite

Like Trump he need please only himself
the sky-engorging balloon of inflated ego
Go tell families with silverware and cars
I, once Cold Mountain, speak what I know

We'll have to change To Fu 杜甫's line to read

It is not mountains and rivers that remain
only the state remains the same
No Mountain said that

Island Inventory

Except for the red-bibbed fox that looks inward
everything faces out toward the waters
in the Edo period you could only get here by boat
a small island no bigger than a flattened rice ball

The four stone lanterns face all directions at once
surrounding them are commemorative stones
one inscribed with the Heart Sutra
a finger pointing at the moon

on most stones, the writing too eroded to read
A small shrine has doors cemented shut
others with empty receptacles, the gods flown
A walkway with a new fence makes a parapet

for flowers, for daffodils, for trees, sal (娑羅双樹) and
sakaki (榊) withered this winter day
for ducks, diving or dabbling, too numerous to name
And the great white heron stalks the waters
one of the Taoist immortals they say

No Mountain on His Contemporaries

Kung 君 was a man of few words

and he never spoke of posterity
If you hide in the woods and caves
they asked how will wisdom be revealed

Kung said you won't wither into wisdom
all those Taoist meditations, sitting on ledges
and in caves will destroy your knees
what wisdom has a man who can't walk to pee

and then there were the Buddha-izers
bobbing like pond ducks to the ringing of a bell
They asked me was I a sympathizer
and I replied, "whatever"

No Mountain Tells of Ueno Wayne

His father drove a gasoline truck
delivering fuel to farm tanks
his mother was a mawworm
who read the texts from her intestines
and prayed for her children's souls

Said he used to feel the burden of family history
a matter he'd received from the generations
part of a compact with his forebearers
made in his name before he was ever born
And now he lets it go by, flotsam on the waters

I spoke and told him my thought
It's in the darkness of their eyes that men get lost

Searching for Wisdom

At the base of the circular library
Ueno Wayne found Jung's Bible
layered in foxed paper and yellowed twine
Each labeled layer was autographed
but was it authentic he asked

Beneath the seventh layer he saw gothic lettering
bold and black –it's his! It is!
he opened the book
beneath the great black leather-bound board
words gifted with gold faces
white winged glyphs of synchronicity

Therein is destiny, said the sage,
not in longevity but in removal
like ducks, he said
we dive and reappear in new places

One Oh One / Ueno Wayne

He recalls the sunny slopes of my childhood
off rabbit hunting on Mount Konochiti
Lake County that was, trout fishing in Kelsey Creek
spearing hitch behind the Clover Creek Dairy

He thought not of immortals but rode the wind
mounted high on fancy's white horse
now homeless sleeping on cardboard
wasted and who will show him the way home

The Taoist Ponders Immortality

I gave up Taoist alchemy, immortality doubtful
our source was Lao-Tzu, that much we knew
after that it was mix and match
we used honey or wine to fry metals
some of them lethal--arsenic, mercury, lead

To make the immortality drink we added crystals
of cinnabar, of barite, of quartz,
of calcite we got from the Wanshan Mine
cinnabar and fake gold were the best
the caldron lent it the heat of mortality

Alchemy's my karma. They call me a man of no doctrine
unclear whether or not I was a monk
except monks don't drink but I do
whether a Buddhist or a Taoist or both
It is not even certain I ever lived but my poems do

三月蚕 / Third Month Silkworms

In the third month the silkworms are still small
Girls come along picking flowers
Against a wall they sport with butterflies
At the pond's edge they skip stones at frogs

They stash plums in their thin silk sleeves
They hack at bamboo sprouts with a golden comb
No matter how hard I think about this
Where they live must be a better home than mine*

* This is the one poem in this book that is a translation. From
p39 of the Iwanami Bunko text. The meaning of the last line
is uncertain.

They look at me, No Mountain
Who is this guy, they say, he's nuts, he talks back
Is something odd in my face or is it
my birch-bark hat or my pigweed staff

They don't understand my words
and I don't use theirs
They glory in being called Drunk Poets
not knowing the first was Li Po 李白

or that no glory's in being drunk or a poet
If you meet a traveler
a person who can understand
please say come to No Mountain

I was thirty years old when poetry came looking for me
I don't know where it came from, from a leaf, a door
it was not a voice and it was not silence
but it touched me, poetry and povety too

I had been a soldier, a courtier, a writer of verse
but I busted my leg and the verse is broken too
counting feet arranging tones, no first person allowed
a mug's game of tic-tac-tootle-doo

Nothing came right, I failed my exams
at home reading books I was bored
I moved to a cave high in the mountains
and began to scribble on the walls of cliffs

it was there three miles high I became Cold Mountain
there Cold Mountain gave me a name
Now I've come down from that mountain
No Mountain is who I am now

The Heart Sutra 般若心経, Gate of No Gate

Bits and q-bits, you ask me, but the Boddhisatva said it
and the Heart Sutra's carved on a stone
on the Isle of Hermits Rest
So be it

All form is like foam; all feelings bubbles, all sensations
mirages
consciousness rides herd on the illusion
so did the Buddha illustrate
the Gateless Gate, the Gate of No Gate

The Great Way is unfenced and gateless,
Once past the checkpoint
You stride across worlds
Like Puss in his seven-league Boots

then the mantra: gate gate pāragate
pārasaṃgate bodhi svāhā,
"gone, gone, everyone gone to the other shore
awakened ones, so be it"

Taoist immortals, the great white cranes
with their red crowns of royalty
glorious doyens of the dance are caged now
Materialists never believe in immortality
so they build their coffins to last a thousand years
What happens when you cage an immortal
you make him no better than a mortal
a mirror image of yourself in the iron cage

The care for externals should lie on the shoulders
like a cloak, it can be thrown aside at any moment
but the cloak become an iron cage at fate's decree
I can see the zoo from my island
In their places are herons, blue grey and white
they stalk silently better than man can devise
they too are masters of stillness

Words for the Birds: An Island Inventory

Benzaiten sole daughter among the Seven Gods
of Happiness, goddess of waters, music, and snakes
plays a lute and waves her magic wand
June's sitar, drip-drop dropping ragas of rain

Among her large retinue swims the tufted duck
a small diver, black except for golden eyes
and with a topknot on the back of his head.
When he dives no one knows where he'll come up

The pochard is a diver too, larger than the tufted
the male red-headed black-breasted and grey-backed
Females make hoarse growls, males have whistles
cut off by a final nasal out of whack-- *aaoo-oo-haa*

The pintail's named for the drake's long tail feathers
Hens make a coarse quack
and they whistle like flutes
depending on the weather

Grebes are short on wings and don't like to fly
Meeting danger they prefer to dive

Lobed toes, good swimmers and divers,
less wary than ducks who're better survivors

Dabblers include the shoveler
a broad spatula beak good for gobbling
Wigeon has a bulbous rear to its head.
no kin of the common pigeon

Spotted-bills throw their tails up-end to feed
The mallard is a showboat with a glossy green head
high necked like those four-story ferries
that wreck leaving hundreds of dead

The white wagtail is a passerine
a musical family, one toe points back and three forward
they perch to sing and are kin to the common sparrow
of which the gods have kindly supplied a plenty
No songster, the wagtail has one good trick
his call is a sharp *chisick-chisick*

The black-headed gulls though raucous in public
are well behaved when they go home
they remove the chicks' shells from the nest
from contention removing the bone

The gallinule also called moorhen, rail, and coot
migrates up to 1500 miles from breeding grounds
in the cold Siberian night

Apart from these family trips, they're not fond of flying
They walk very well on their strong legs
the long toes grab a grassblade and drain it to the dregs

The great cormorant's name goes better in Greek
phalacros corax, the bald crow, bald as a buzzard
cormorant fishing practiced in China Korea Japan
They're dumb as a sack of hammers
If you don't want them to swallow the catch
just put a ring around their gizzard

Rapacious officials and crafty are crows
no immortals among them just bureaucrats
ambitious for the prime ministerial privilege
and the ripe garbage bags at Nagata-cho[5]

---

5. 永田町: where the national government sits.

The door to the house I once lived in
became trellised with vines
through them I watched those time travelers
the sun and the moon but never saw
men become ghosts, never saw one immortal
or a crane carrying someone away on its back

We studied geomancy, "the science of the sand"
graveyards outside the north or west gates of the city
to protect from bandits, invaders, and floods that befall
look beyond the city walls
the ancient graves are plowed into fields
Now you know why I moved to No Mountain

Editorial note:
        In Renaissance magic, geomancy was classified as
one of the seven "forbidden arts", along
with necromancy, hydromancy, aeromancy, pyromancy,
chiromancy (palmistry), and spatulamancy (scapulimancy).
The Arabs called it the "science of the sand."

Shinobazu Pond's a lotus pond
as even in winter dried stalks attest
like a litter of broken crane legs but
come June it will burst into bloom

A lotus pond's an auspicious place
for a crane to pick up a Taoist hitchhiker
thumbing across the galaxies of time
bound for the Isles of the Blest

I'm hoping to meet a buddha
If you can grasp my verses
you may be the buddha or what's no worse
maybe his father or mother

A man versed in the arts
of music, archery, writing, charioteering,
and math, in all of the rites bespoke
blown east and west, drifting like duckweed
I come from Poor and my name is Broke

When I died I went first to Mt. Taishan
abode of departed spirits
the geomancy there's sublime
graves dating back to the neolithic
gravel and dirt and the smell of time

Hard on the trail even now
I'm climbing Lotus Peak again
to wait once more for birdland
the wind-tossed winter moon
the lantern of a solitary crane

We did not call ourselves Chinese
we were the 漢人 Han-jen, the People of Han

our coins had holes in their centers
as till recently had the five-yen coin in Japan

That way we could string them together
to make up larger sums
Our world was surrounded by a ring
of iron bearing mountains

The homeless people I know in the park
don't practice the profession of homelessness
they don't practice anything
they just are

I watch the mud-ball of my mind
for a lotus to flower from the mire

The Marquise de Tai, Lady Ch'eng

Let me tell you about the Marquise de Tai
A lady so lovely diamonds shrank from her toes
otherwise known as the Lady Ch'eng
she lived some two thousand years ago

and of course given her early glamor
she wanted to be robed in it through eternity
and be admired among the glorious
Taoist gods of immortality

They dug her up a few decades back
well preserved after two thousand years
hermetically sealed in mercury salts
helped by the dry Hunan atmosphere

Dead at fifty looking like chewed up sugarcane
Of teeth she had 16 in her mouth, badly worn
in her belly 136 mushmelon seeds from a final meal
A gallstone blocked the end of her bile tract

Her arteries clogged with plaque Lady Tai
died when biliary distress caused a heart attack
We have disaster because we have a body, said Lao-Tsu
Pretty girls make graves, much later added Kerouac

Late January sun the reapers have come
reaping the broken cordage of the lotus stalks
the carnage of brown and broken stems
broken like the legs of cranes and herons

broken like the lines of my verse
a jumble of wasp's waists and crane's knees
and I can't keep my tones straight or flat
the men come in rafts and gather the roughage
piling it high on the pond banks
like the shambles after a battle

around me now the water's clear and calm
and the divers return to sup,
head first with their tails in the air
their feathered butts sticking strait up

this was writ in the year of the rat
mid-way in the winter than never quit

Gathas are but Buddhist doggerel the poets insist
gathas or poems what's the uproar
say I write bundles of 'em on bamboo sticks
take one home with you, I've got more

Gathas sum up sutras
I have 'em like frogs have spawn
short-hand signs like mudras
join me below No Mountain's pond

You won't see No Mountain though
nor will sore eyes see Ueno's mount
back above us is Suribachi-yama*
a royal burial mound for Known-no-more

After the rain the puddles reflect the sky
look down to see the clouds go by
gate gate pāragate, pārasaṃgate,
gone, gone, everyone gone to the other shore

*摺鉢山

Books save no one from death
nor will they free us from want
those who can't read wish they could
those who can don't regret it

Are the literate better than others
a man who can't read has a world in his head
and doesn't have to look things up
Does he find peace? The literate think so

Tolstoy's story of Ivan Ilyich
talks about this. I wish I could read his books--
the thought of all the books I've never read
the thought of one like me, a thousand years dead

Writing hints at immortality
words of the ancients proclaim and shout it
I once wrote it's not certain I ever lived
but my poems do. Today I doubt it

A thief visited our island today
it was a snake day, an open gate
he copped the five-yen coins from the shrines
emptied the offertory box into his pocket
and went off with some fresh rice cakes

Had it been a homeless person, who'd care?
A tom cat who eats the offered tofu
because of his hunger--
that's just ecology, giving to the needy
as the Buddha told us we should

But this man though ugly as Enma
wore clean clothes and a gold watch and ring
He forgot the Blue-Faced Shōmen-Kongō[6]
who watches over what comes to pass
sees every wrong and forgets nothing

I watched the theft unfold, spoke no sass
one day old Yama'll stick a red-hot poker up his ass

---

6. 青面金剛

Enma

Ueno Daibutsu / 上野大仏

Descended up north in Echigo 1631
he's looked on wars and turmoils
gone under earthquakes suffered fire and flood
gave his body's plates to make airplane parts
now only his face is left

The archaic smile suggests no Cheshire grin
a somber upturn of thin lips is all there is
the hooded eyes that have looked
on what is past or passing or to come
we can't fall any farther than that, say the students

The daibutsu is the full moon in the sky
reflected in the pond that's your mind, I exclaim
Later they come to give thanks
for having passed their entrance exams

Wayne Goes West

Sunday Nozomi Super Gō to Osaka
meeting old friends again
missing Mt. Fuji again after fifteen years
gray rain, gray sky, the trees are gray

Asahi Shinbun has no "Poems Time to Time"[7]
he'd always used for *uranai*[8]
No view of Fuji, best seen this way sd Basho
she's most herself when she doesn't show

Old friend goes west from Kō-kaku-rō 黄鶴楼

Smoke-flowers blur over the river
until only the river is seen
the long Kiang, reaching heaven[9]

---

7. Poems Time to Time": Ori-Ori no Uta 折々のうた.

8. Divination.
9. Reworked from Ezra Pound's "Separation on the River
Kiang." Yes, Pound didn't know that "Kiang" meant river.
Even so, the line has resonance.

Kōshin (庚申)'s Island

Yasha / Kōshin / Shōmenkongō /
placed at crossroads, graveyard gates and shrines
Wanting acceptance from the Xian west
Meiji puritans banned the belief as "pagan"

A little island not made by hands
ice sheets left it here when they subsided
unlike the bigger island with its shrine
ordered up to suit the mighty Ieyasu

In Kōshin monkeys bear away our sins
beats loading them on a god's only begotten
and sacrificing the lamb. Not paganism but taoism,
the ancientest religion known to man

can quell those three death bugs (三尸) in our flesh
monkeys and men--differing shades of the primal dust

Kōshin, Guardian of Crossroads and Gates

In the human body lurk three corpse-worms
viral parasites that put the reek in our shit
demon bugs that hasten the death of their host
begetters of rumors and gossip

It is these Kōshin's three monkeys oppose
See-no-evil, hear-no-evil, speak-no-evil
you will find them along the base of his statue
scotching the gossip that rots village life

Mouth, ears, and eyes are gates to our inner gnomes
The cure is reciting sutras every sixty days
else the bugs report your gossip and shorten your life
evil and *live* are palindromes

Electronic villages replace the old ones only dafter
Facebook YouTube Instagram, Twitter Tumblr Telegram
are the viral kings--*corona* means crown:
Jack fell down, broke his, and Jill came tumbling after

Time beings get raddled on the road
They don't know that
their own minds are the Buddha

If they knew that they wouldn't seek him
outside their minds

Prior to his Nirvana
Buddha told his disciples
Be lamps unto yourselves

their minds
those pearls wrapped in rags

Adapted from Red Pine, notes 210, 214 and 247

Miao Miao

Yang Hsui was a great hand
at solving muddles
He solved one around the year 200
for Ts'ao Ts'ao

When the characters for shao (young)
and nu (woman) are combined
the result is miao, meaning mystery

Later a multi-volume work on gynecology
Ancient & modern Acupuncture
& Moxibustion Methods was compiled by
the polynomial Qin Fu Zhen Jiu Miao

*First two stanzas based on Red Pine's footnote 144, p.
132.*

I wedded once No Mountain says
sought titles sweet and triumphs
had houses lands prestige
and knew the way to dance with a woman
And gave these up for a hermitage? No--

I dream of arms like the famished dream of food
stir your cream in my coffee sweet doll
I'll be your sugar daddy
if you'll be my jelly roll

Sweet sixteen is the age they sing about
but I once sent a poem to a woman aged fifty-three
told her I wanted to be the parakeet
picking flowers in her cherry tree

She chopped me down like an old fig tree
cute, she sd, to be so antique
and went waltzing on her way
serving the miao of sisterhood and mystery

In Cold Hell and Thicket

Po-cha or *po-po-cha-cha*
transliterates Sanskrit *Ababa*
the cold hell of frozen tongue and lips
ababa the only sound they can make

no bridge across the Ocean of Impermanence
wu-wei, doing nothing, that's one way
and this whiff of a woman's thicket
what can I say

You ask me how I came here
was it inspiration
No, I cut a forked stick
and used divination

Thirty spokes converge on a hub
but it's the emptiness that makes a wheel work
You may read this thinking No Mountain knows
but he knows less than an ignorant elf

Be lamps unto yourselves.

The Dead Revisit the Pond

On a day of lost words, August,
92 degrees at 4 o'clock and the mercury's stopped.
Again the nymphs[10] have come up from Tellus,
Males of fourteen species shaking their timbals.

The cicadas are chanting sutras
Drumming, intoning the sacred texts.
They sing as they die in the attic,
And the difference is this: they know it.

The poem might come to us in sleep like
The dead who visit the pond at night.
It's a day without words, August.
It might be raining but it's not.

---

10. In biology, a *nymph* is the immature form of insects such
as cicadas.

No Mountain Bids Farewell

Life is motion, an old poet said
and everywhere weather, weather
Mid-March the trees put on their wedding gowns
around the pond and up the mountain sides

The rhyme of bamboo and pine
the wind lilting in the willows
Double sunsets linger to bless
one in the east windows, one in the west

You may read me thinking No Mountain knows
but his bookshelves are empty
Be lamps unto yourselves
and as to what will be, only the viruses know

They say we tread a narrow way
by Tophet flare to Judgement Day
Sing me a song, old toad
help me down Cemetery Road

Sources

Chung, Ling. "Han Shan, *Dharma Bums*, and Charles
    Frazier's *Cold Mountain*." *Comparative
    Literature Studies*, 48 No. 4 (2011): 541-65.

入矢義高『寒山』中国詩人選集第 5 巻　岩波書店
    昭和 33年。Iriya, Yoshitaka. Kanzan. *Selections
    from Chinese Poetry,* vol. 5. Iwanami Shoten,
    1956.

Mori Ogai. "Kanzan Jittoku." *The Incident at Sakai and
    other stories*: Vol 1 of *The Historical Literature
    of Mori Ogai*. Trans. David Dilworth and Thomas
    Rimer. Honolulu: Hawaii UP, 1977.

Ohnuki-Tierney, Emiko. *The Monkey as Mirror:
    Symbolic Transformations in Japanese History
    and Ritual*. New Jersey: Princeton University
    Press, 1987.
Red Pine. *The Collected Songs of Cold Mountain*. Rev.
    ed. Port Townsend, WA: Copper Canyon Press,
    1990.

Snyder, Gary. *Rip Rap and Cold Mountain Poems*. San Francisco: North Point Press, 1990.

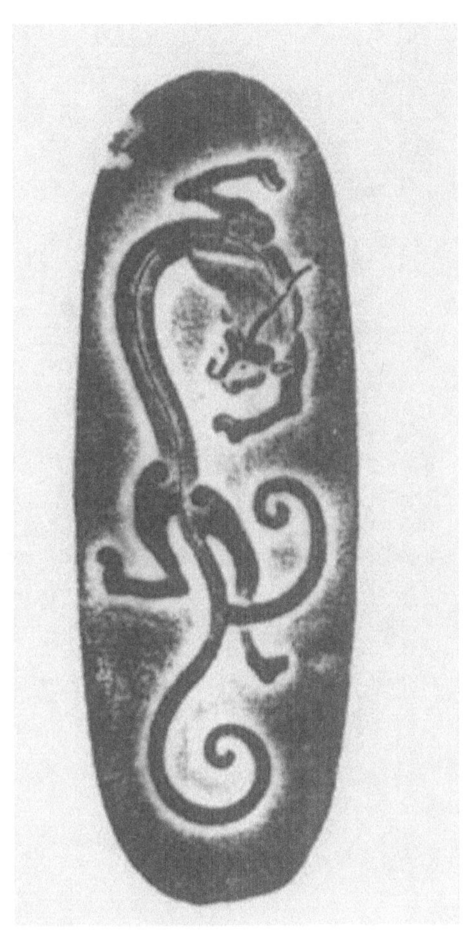